P9-BVH-482

Water Can Be...

by Laura Purdie Salas

illustrations by Violeta Dabija

MILLBROOK PRESS • MINNEAPOLIS

For my parents, Jimmy and Dorothy
Purdie—canoers, skiers, swimmers…
lovers of water —L.P.S.

To my son Daniel, for being the light
of my life —V.D.

Millbrook Press
A division of Lerner Publishing Group, Inc.
241 First Avenue North
Minneapolis, MN 55401 USA

Website address: www.lernerbooks.com

Main body text set in GFY Brutus 28/42.
Typeface provided by The Chank Company.

Library of Congress Cataloging-in-Publication Data

Salas, Laura Purdie.
    Water can be . . . / by Laura Purdie Salas ; illustrations by Violeta Dabija.
        p.   cm
    Summary: This picture book poetically explores the many things water can
be—from home maker and ship breaker to cloud fluffer and fire snuffer. Back
matter provides additional explanations.
    ISBN 978-1-4677-0591-2 (lib. bdg. : alk. paper)
    ISBN 978-1-4677-2539-2 (eBook)
    1. Water—Juvenile literature. I. Dabija, Violeta, illustrator. II. Title.
GB662.3.S25 2014
553.7—dc23   2013017772

Manufactured in the United States of America
1 – DP – 12/31/13

Water is water—
it's puddle, pond, sea.
When springtime comes splashing,
the water flows free.

Water can be a...

Tadpole hatcher

Picture catcher

Otter feeder

Downhill speeder

Garden soaker

Valley cloaker

Thirst quencher

Kid drencher

Drink cooler

Rainbow jeweler

Home maker

Ship breaker

Water is water—
it's fog, frost, and sea.
When autumn comes chasing,
water can be a...

Cloud fluffer

Fire snuffer

School drink-er

Bruise shrinker

Salmon highway

Eagle flyway

Storm creator

Decorator

Woodchuck warmer

Snowman former

Water is water—
it's ice, snow, and sea.
Now go and discover
what else it can be!

More about Water

Water is everywhere! Sometimes you notice it, like when you get a drink or take a bath. But water also does things you might not realize. Water creates fog and snow, makes plants grow, and keeps all living things on Earth alive.

Tadpole hatcher: Most frogs and toads lay eggs in ponds. When the eggs hatch, tadpoles are born. Tadpoles live in the water for a few weeks or months until they change into frogs or toads. Then they live mostly on land.

Picture catcher: When a pond or a puddle is calm, it can act like a mirror. A lake might show the trees onshore, or a puddle might show your face!

Otter feeder: A healthy river is full of fish. Lots of animals both in and out of the river rely on the river for their food. River otters love to eat fish. They'll also dine on turtles, frogs, salamanders, and crayfish.

Downhill speeder: In spring, water from melted snow flows down mountains. The water can turn gentle creeks into wild rapids!

Garden soaker: Plants need sunshine, soil, and water to grow. Rain is an important part of the water cycle. Rain falls from the sky and flows to the oceans. Then water near the ocean's surface turns into a gas called water vapor. It floats up into the sky and then turns into water droplets. Each droplet coats a speck of dust, and many droplets together make a cloud. Those clouds rain on Earth, and the whole water cycle continues!

Valley cloaker: Water can turn into a gas called water vapor. When a lot of water vapor is in the air, fog might form. The water vapor condenses, which means it turns back into liquid water. The tiny liquid water droplets wrap around bits of dust in the air. They hover near the ground, forming fog.

Thirst quencher: Every animal on Earth needs water, including humans. Without water, we could not sweat or go to the bathroom. Our blood, which is mostly water, could not do its important jobs. Our bodies are more than half water!

Kid drencher: Whether you splash in the waves or jump through a sprinkler, water makes a summer day better (and wetter)!

Drink cooler: When water is 32°F (0°C) or colder, it turns into ice. Ice is handy for lots of things, such as cooling your drinks in summer or making a surface for ice-skating in winter.

Rainbow jeweler: Did you know that without water, we would have no rainbows? They form when sunshine meets water vapor in the air. The sunlight hits the water vapor, bends, and travels to your eye. The light makes different colors depending on how it bends.

Home maker: Oceans cover more than two-thirds of Earth's surface. Many plants and animals, such as fish, crabs, algae, turtles, and octopuses, live around coral reefs. Most reefs form in clear, shallow, warm water. Some of a reef's plants and animals use the sunlight that shines through the water to make food and oxygen.

Ship breaker: Water is powerful and sometimes destructive. Floods, hurricanes, and tsunamis are all dangerous. During an ocean storm, waves out at sea can climb 30 feet (9 meters) tall.

Cloud fluffer: Clouds are made of water droplets that are so tiny they float! During the day, clouds can help cool Earth by blocking some of the sun's energy and heat. At night, they are like a blanket. They trap the sun's heat near the ground and keep Earth warm.

Fire snuffer: Water can put out a fire. It cools a fire off, and it also blocks the fire's air supply. (Fire needs oxygen from the air so it can burn.)

School drink-er: Water fountains are everywhere. Grab a quick drink when you walk down the hall. It's good for you!

Bruise shrinker: Ouch! Sprained ankles and bruises hurt! If you press a cloth filled with ice against your injury, it keeps some of your blood (inside your body) from rushing to the part that's hurt. That keeps your skin from swelling and bruising as much.

Salmon highway: Most salmon hatch in streams and then swim to the ocean. They live there for several years. Then they swim back upstream to lay eggs where they were born. Some salmon swim hundreds of miles to return home.

Eagle flyway: Many bald eagles and other birds in Canada and the northern United States fly south each winter to nest or find food where it's warmer. Some birds follow rivers like they are maps. The Mississippi River is called the Mississippi Flyway. Birds can follow its path and not get lost. And a fish dinner is always nearby!

Storm creator: Water is part of most storms. Rain, sleet, snow, and hail are all made of some form of water.

Decorator: When it's very cold outside and very warm and moist inside, frost might form on your windows. Frost is water vapor that has frozen into ice crystals. These tiny pieces of ice can look like feathers or curlicues because of the way the ice crystals form on the glass. It's like winter making art on your windows!

Woodchuck warmer: Snow is cold, but it can help keep things warm! Snow has a lot of air trapped in it, and it is like a cozy coat for the animals and plants underneath it. Woodchucks (also known as groundhogs) feast all summer and then sleep all winter in underground burrows. The snow above keeps their burrows from becoming dangerously cold.

Snowman former: You can build lots of things from snow, like balls, forts, and sliding hills. And it's always fun to make a cheery snowman or snow family!

Glossary

condense: turn from water vapor into liquid water

coral reef: an ocean structure built by coral animals that is home to many other sea creatures

frost: a powdery type of ice that forms on things in cold weather. Frost is water vapor that has frozen into ice crystals.

hatch: to be born from an egg

ice crystal: a small piece of ice that has many sides

otter: a brown, furry animal with webbed feet that lives in or near water

oxygen: a gas that humans and animals need to breathe. There is oxygen in the air and in water.

quench: to end thirst by drinking something

sleet: frozen or partly frozen rain

snuff: to put out a fire

tadpole: the creature that hatches from a frog or toad egg

upstream: the direction opposite the flow of water in a river or stream

valley: lower land between hills or mountains

water vapor: water that has turned into a gas

woodchuck: a small, furry animal that lives underground

Further Reading

Bullard, Lisa. *Watch Over Our Water.* Minneapolis: Millbrook Press, 2012.

Just Add Water: Science Experiments You Can Sink, Squirt, Splash, Sail. New York: Children's Press, 2008.

Lyon, George Ella. *All the Water in the World.* New York: Atheneum Books for Young Readers, 2011.

Strauss, Rochelle. *One Well: The Story of Water on Earth.* Toronto: Kids Can Press, 2007.

Waldman, Neil. *The Snowflake: A Water Cycle Story.* Minneapolis: Millbrook Press, 2003.